Backpacking

The Ultimate Guide to getting started on
your first backpacking trip

Timothy S. Morris

Table of Contents

OK, So You Want to Go Backpacking Huh?

Do you have a sudden itch to venture out into the wilderness, wake up next to a babbling brook somewhere and watch the sun slowly come over the horizon? Are you ready to escape (albeit temporarily) from the daily grind and a society that prioritizes consumerism over all else?

If so, you may be thinking that backpacking is an excellent way to accomplish all these things and you would be right. Whether it's just for a weekend or for a month-long adventure, backpacking in the wilderness is an excellent way to shed the stresses of modern life allowing us to become one with nature.

If you think that sounds slightly mystical you'd be right again. The truth, however, is that backpacking really does spark something inside us — a primal connection with the land that is impossible to duplicate by performing any other recreational activity.

If you have ever been camping before, you may have experienced this feeling already but rest assured that backpacking is the single best way to experience the wilderness as it's meant to be experienced. Think about it this way: when we drive through an area — whether a scenic National Park or a vast seascape along the coast — we see the beauty as if it were a postcard framed in the vehicle window.

Truly experiencing these beautiful and awe-inspiring places requires that we get out of the car and put one foot in front of the other. Only by walking through one of these places are we able to connect with the landscape and in some way actually become part of it.

Backpacking is an amazing activity. It lets us experience natural beauty that is simply inaccessible by vehicle or ATV. We are able to reconnect with our primitive human selves while getting some serious exercise at the same time.

The problem for many of us, however, is getting started. Finding a good place to backpack, selecting gear (one trip to the sporting goods store makes this seem like an overwhelming feat by itself) and learning how to survive without the modern amenities we have come to rely on are all daunting tasks for the inexperienced backpacker.

The good news is that you are reading this book. That means you have an interest in heading out into the woods. That is the most important thing and probably the one thing I **cannot** teach you in this guide. For everything else, this book has the answers.

If you are looking for a solid, no-fluff guide to getting into and out of the woods safely using only the gear carried on your back, look no further than this book. Combining years of backpacking experience I have compiled the information you need to know when traveling by foot in the Great Outdoors. Whether it's just a quick weekend outing or you are preparing to traverse one of the many amazing long-distance trails in the country, you will know exactly what it takes to make backpacking the enjoyable and enlightening experience it is meant to be.

So, let's not waste anymore time and get started...

Chapter One: Preparation and Fitness

Traveling through the wilderness alone or in a group is a dangerous undertaking. Make no mistake — backpacking is an extremely rewarding experience, but it can quickly bring us to our knees and even threaten our very survival if we don't take the time to plan for our adventure.

Walking long distances requires cardiovascular fitness (unless, of course, you want the memory of your trip to be nothing more than a pounding heart and lungs gasping for air). This doesn't mean we need to join a gym and start an intensive workout routine. Rather, simply walking with a pack on is enough training to ensure our bodies are ready for the stress and strain often encountered during a backpacking trip.

This is known as specific training because it trains the body in the very thing you want to accomplish. If you want to condition your body to climb long distances carrying a heavy load, what better way to train than to *climb long distances with a heavy load.* This is good news because it means you don't have to live near a wilderness area to get into shape for backpacking.

Many times when training for an adventure I simply throw on my pack loaded with gear and walk around town. Even just a few miles a day is enough to prepare your body for the strain of backpacking. If you already walk or jog for exercise you're halfway there. Just throw a backpack on with some weight in it and work out as you normally would. The additional weight helps strengthen your legs and condition your cardiovascular system for the conditions likely to be encountered on the trail.

You should start exercising **now**. You can't expect to get fit for backpacking in a couple days or a couple weeks (although lots of people try). In fact, some people think they will get into shape with the first few days on the trail. The reality is that these individuals often struggle with aches, pains and cramps throughout the entire trip and fail to enjoy the experience as they should. Don't be one of those people!

Even if you haven't exercised in years, start small but start now.

Walking Is an Art

We don't often think about walking. It's just one of those things we learn at a young age and do throughout our lives without giving it much thought at all. A successful backpacker, however, has mastered the art of walking. Although this concept may seem foreign to you now, believe me when I tell you that there are few things that feel better on the trail than finding that perfect stride.

The perfect stride is when walking requires seemingly no energy and the miles simply melt away. When you find the right stride (which often varies based on pack load and terrain among other factors) it's like you become part of the trail; effortlessly gliding along the terrain.

The wrong stride, on the other hand, can be torture. Whether it's because you are trying to walk too fast to keep up with others in your group or you are carrying too heavy of a pack, the wrong stride is guaranteed to make your trip unenjoyable and even worse...it could lead to injury.

Finding the proper stride is simply a matter of practice. Take it easy: backpacking is not a race. It's about enjoying your surroundings and taking in the natural beauty all around you.

Walking is a dynamic activity. By that I mean that one day the perfect stride could net you 15 miles per day and the next day it could be cut in half. The key is to listen to your body and learn from it as you go.

A word of warning: There are sure to be days on the trail when finding that perfect stride seems impossible; when no matter how hard you try every mile seems like an eternity. It's OK and it happens to all of us from time to time. On days like that it's usually best to take it easy, relax a little and remind yourself that the adventure is found right where you are, not at some imaginary finish line.

One tip that often works when you are having trouble finding a rhythm is to chant (out loud if you have to) any words that come into your head. It could be a song, a poem or some nonsensical gibberish as long as it has a steady rhythm. Moving your feet to this chant can often lead to finding an economical walking stride when all other methods fail.

Planning Without Overthinking It

Like so many other things we do in life, a backpacking trip requires planning. Some of the details may be hard to figure out exactly without experience such as how much distance you can cover in a day or exactly how much food you should bring, but there are some general rules to follow that are pretty accurate.

Obviously, you can adjust these figures as your experience and confidence grow. Probably the most important concept to understand when planning a backpacking trip is to give yourself enough time to complete the journey comfortably. Deciding on a hike that requires you to make 25 miles every single day just to make it back to your car in time for work on Monday isn't the way to plan an adventure.

If anything, plan on making worse time than you can possibly imagine. That allows more time for sightseeing, enjoying the trip and any unforeseen circumstances like inclement weather, injury or a trail detour not found on any of your maps.

How Far Can You Go?

Although backpacking isn't a race, it is important to account for speed while planning a trip. You need to know approximately how much terrain you can cover in a day (on average) so you can plan the trip according to how much time you have available for backpacking and any other commitments you have outside of the wilderness.

While many factors affect how far you can walk on a daily basis including physical ability, pack weight, terrain, etc. you can estimate your speed per day using some generic figures that work well for most people.

Play it safe and assume that on an average day you will walk 10-12 miles. As your experience and fitness level improve you can probably walk this far before lunch assuming relatively easy terrain, but these numbers represent a good baseline for any novice backpacker. Please feel free to adjust these numbers according to your personal fitness level and experience walking long distances, but it's better to arrive at your destination a day early than it is to be three days behind. People back home may start wondering where you are and there have been many instances where a hiker is thought to be missing (think Search & Rescue teams combing through the forest) when in fact the individual was perfectly fine but behind a few days from his or her original hiking plan.

Know Where You're Going

Travelers in the old days didn't have the luxury of perfectly scaled maps that detail every twist and turn of the trail. In many cases, these people used the sun and stars as their primary navigational aid; often cutting trails through virgin land as they went.

Today, we don't have to worry about such things. There are multiple sources for excellent quality maps specifically designed for backpackers. These maps often include useful information such as designated campsites, secondary trails and other invaluable resources.

High-quality maps and other information are available for most popular areas. A good place to start is Google. Using Maps you can hone in on a specific area where you would like to hike and from there contact local resource centers for up-to-date information and maps specific to the area. The National Forest Service, Bureau of Land Management (BLM) and the National Park Service are all excellent resources more than happy to share information with backpackers.

Another often overlooked resource is other backpackers. If you are thinking of hiking in a specific area, try to find others who have also hiked the area. Often these people are an invaluable resource that can share local knowledge not found on any map. A trail obstruction, for instance, won't be on the map and could theoretically add half a day worth of hiking to your route. Someone who recently hiked this trail can provide you with this type of information.

As a novice backpacker you may have trouble locating other hikers to discuss your proposed route with (but don't worry — you will meet plenty of new friends on the trail). Modern technology comes to the rescue. There are countless online discussion forums dedicated to backpacking and membership is almost always free. Take a few minutes to set up an account and talk with some of the hikers online. Most of these people are more than willing to share information with a fellow outdoor enthusiast. Just make sure you are honest about your inexperience and usually someone can steer you in the right direction with helpful tips tailored to your proposed trip.

Also, don't forget about your vehicle. Many trails meander around before eventually coming back to where you started. Others — especially popular long distance trails like the Pacific Crest Trail (PCT) and Appalachian Trail — leave you thousands of miles from where you started.

Make sure you have a ride if you plan on exiting the woods from a different location or arrange in advance to leave a secondary vehicle at your planned exit point. Few things can be more frustrating than trying to bum a ride after a tiring week spent hiking in the high country.

Permits

Most places you are likely to hike do not require a permit but some of the more popular destinations such as National Parks do. In some cases, availability of these permits is extremely limited; often requiring you to apply months in advance.

If you plan on traveling through an area where permits are required, reach out to the local office responsible for managing the land (i.e. BLM, NPS or NFS) to apply. Permits can even be applied for online for many popular destinations.

You're Not a Pro...Yet

Even the best planning cannot prepare you for many of the challenges typically experienced on the trail. The best way to learn is through experience and one of the best ways to get yourself into trouble (or at very least have a horrible trip) is biting off more than you can chew in the beginning.

In other words, don't plan on making your first trip a complete trek of the PCT (2,600 miles) because it's not gonna happen. Instead, start small. Take a weekend trip or two followed by successively longer adventures. This allows your body time to acclimate to the backpacking life while teaching you many valuable lessons along the way.

Don't worry, it won't be too long before you're itching to tackle the big three National Scenic Trails — otherwise known as the Triple Crown — which includes the Pacific Crest Trail, the Appalachian Trail and the Continental Divide Trail. The important thing is to learn while you build up to these extremely challenging (but totally gratifying) adventures.

Backpacking is like that. Once you're hooked, you always want to keep pushing yourself to see new places and experience new things. It's certainly a lifestyle worth pursuing as long as you take the time to prepare before heading onto the trail.

Chapter Two: Weight is Your Enemy

No, I'm not talking about *your* weight (although backpacking is a great way to get into shape). The weight of your gear is one of the most important factors. In fact, it is one of those things that can literally ruin an otherwise perfectly planned trip.

Packing gear for a trip — whether it is a two day outing or two month adventure — requires as much, if not more, planning than the rest of the trip combined. When you take into account the often high costs associated with quality backpacking gear, it only makes sense to take your time selecting equipment.

Every ounce saved matters and there are quite a few accomplished hikers who subscribe to the ultralight philosophy of backpacking. That is to say they become so fanatical about the weight of gear that they often forgo certain comforts in an effort to keep their packs as light as possible.

That's **not** what I suggest you do however. While ultralight backpacking can be a rewarding experience, most of us will do well to find a good balance between weight and comfort. Your hiking experiences will be much more enjoyable and the *extremely* high cost associated with much of today's ultralight gear are enough to send most of us running back to our couches and TV sets without giving backpacking another thought.

Although we will discuss gear in detail throughout this book, there are three things you should consider whenever shopping for a new piece of gear: performance, durability and weight.

Performance refers to a piece of gear's ability to perform as intended. A rain jacket isn't any good if it isn't waterproof just as a stove isn't worthwhile if it doesn't cook food, right?

We always want to select items that work well. Online product reviews are an excellent way to learn about how a product actually functions compared with what the manufacturer claims it does.

Likewise, durability is also important. If you're forking over $150 for a good internal frame backpack you want to be assured that the equipment is constructed in such a way as to provide years of faithful service.

When it comes to durability, online reviews can also be helpful. Purchasing name brand items with a proven reputation for quality and durability is also a good idea, especially when it comes to essential items such as your pack, sleeping bag and tent.

Finally, the weight of every item in your pack needs to be considered. A difference of one ounce may not seem like a big deal, but let me tell you, those ounces add up! A few ounces here, a few ounces there and next thing you know the pack weighs 70 pounds when it could have weighed 50 pounds had you spent the time researching product weights before the purchase.

Also, don't always believe the manufacturer when they tell you what a product weighs. Although these estimates are usually accurate, there are exceptions. My recommendation is to bring a small scale to the sporting goods store with you and weigh any item you are considering.

This may seem like a lot of work but a difference of only 10 pounds on a long walk can be a huge difference, especially when traversing rough terrain and near the end of the journey.

How much weight you carry depends on how long you will be gone, whether or not you go alone (multiple people can split the weight of essential items) and how many comfort items you decide to bring.

Before even considering gear remember this: you must add approximately two pounds of weight per day for food and fuel and one pound for every pint of water carried. Especially on long hikes, food, fuel and water are likely to be most of the weight so it again makes sense to keep the weight of other gear to a minimum whenever possible.

As a general rule when solo hiking, total gear weight should be no more than 25-30 pounds. Once food and water is added to this, the pack should come in around 50 pounds assuming a two-week trip. Although this isn't an extreme amount of weight (when properly distributed with a good pack), 50 pounds is still a lot of weight; especially for a novice backpacker. Of course, a weekend trip should allow for much lighter pack weights and more importantly, these weekend trips allow you to experiment with different gear combinations to find that perfect balance between functionality and weight on the trail.

Pack Rat Syndrome

One of the most rewarding parts of backpacking is that we learn how little we actually need to survive. No TV, no comfortable couch and no refrigerator full of goodies.

The human race is a bunch of pack rats. I'm not singling anyone out here — we are all guilty of it. From storing unnecessary items at home to trying to fit too many things into a backpack, it's human nature to store things that we *think we might need at some point*. While it's important to think ahead when planning gear for a trip, it's important to realize that we cannot take everything we need for every possible situation we might encounter.

What we need is a solid base of equipment (see Appendix I). From this base we can add and remove items depending on the area of the hike and the weather. You likely don't need a heavy winter coat if hiking at low elevation in the summer, for instance. But if you plan on hiking in the desert you'll need to carry more water than you would in an area full of natural water sources. Again, experience and proper planning are the way to learn what works and what doesn't firsthand.

Humans are pack rats for another reason too. It's an unspoken truth within the backpacking community that you **will** fill your pack no matter how big or small it is. This is important because a weekend hike doesn't require a massive internal frame pack but rest assured that if that's what you're using you will find a way to fill it.

For this reason, it's usually a good idea to purchase a pack just large enough for the type of backpacking you plan to do. Most experienced hikers have multiple packs depending on the amount of gear they need to carry and how long they plan to be gone.

If all you have is one pack, shoot for something in the 40-60L range. While most people would agree that this is overkill for a weekend excursion, it is large enough for distance hikes without being overly large and heavy thus providing a versatile pack that can be used for a variety of hikes large and small.

In the following chapters you will learn about specific types of gear and various options within each category. Please remember to always choose the lightest options available within your budget (most of the time lighter means more expensive in the backpacking world).

Chapter Three: Don't Skimp on Footwear

One of the most unpleasant parts of backpacking, especially over long distances, is the wear and tear on your feet. Fortunately, this issue can be mitigated with proper footwear.

Think about it: you are carrying a heavy load on your back which is evenly distributed across your upper body. Unfortunately, your feet still have to carry all that weight over varying terrain. Footwear not designed to provide comfort and support while hiking can quickly lead to blisters, infection and overall discomfort on the trail.

The footwear you select should also take into account the weather likely to be encountered during the trip. I know plenty of backpackers perfectly content hiking in sandals during the summer, but this choice obviously wouldn't be appropriate while trudging through a snow-covered trail in winter.

We just got finished talking about weight but there is something else you should consider specifically when shopping for footwear. Studies have proven that **one pound of weight on your foot is equal to five pounds of weight on your back**. Think about that for a moment...

And since you are just getting into backpacking as a hobby, let's take the brutal winter hikes off the table for the time being. There will be plenty of time to strap snowshoes, crampons and an ice axe to your pack in the future. For now, let's focus on mild weather backpacking.

That means you do not need heavy hiking boots with insulation, waterproof membranes and everything else. In fact, you don't need boots at all.

Ankle Support is a Myth

Most of us have heard that wearing footwear with a high cut is good for ankle support. You may be thinking this is especially important when backpacking since you will have extra weight on your back while traveling over rough terrain.

I'm telling you right now that a hiking boot does not provide ankle support anymore than a good pair of running shoes does. The thin layer of leather or synthetic fabric isn't going to support anything.

What does provide ankle support? The heel cup of the shoe or boot. That is why many hikers choose lightweight hiking shoes or sandals when trekking in mild weather. They provide adequate support while still allowing your feet to breathe and move naturally. That is the type of footwear you need to avoid injury and uncomfortably sweaty feet.

In mild weather, my footwear of choice is either a pair of hiking sneakers (basically lightweight running shoes with improved grip on the bottom of the sole) or hiking sandals. Either choice is good because they provide support for the foot while protecting it from sharp objects on the trail without being heavy or hot.

Lightweight hiking boots are also a good choice — especially the three season models commonly available — because they provide a lightweight option that is good even when the weather is less than ideal.

Make Like Cinderella and Try On the Shoe!

Although I am usually a proponent of shopping online for good deals, the shoes or boots you use while hiking should NEVER be purchased online. You cannot possibly ensure a proper fit when browsing through images on the Internet.

You need to spend some time (a few hours if necessary) to find the shoes or boots that fit your feet properly. Any slippage, pressure points or parts of the shoe that aren't completely comfortable will be exponentially worse on the trail. Many a backpacking trip has been outright ruined simply because someone didn't take the time to select appropriate footwear.

The best way to do this is to shop at a store specializing in outdoor gear. The staff are usually very knowledgeable and often these locations have special equipment available that allows you to test the fit of a particular shoe at an incline to see how it feels. Trust your own judgement when it comes to finding what works and what doesn't but the employees at these stores are typically invaluable when it comes to selecting footwear and other essential gear.

And don't forget to keep the weight of the shoe in mind at all times! The lighter, the better.

Socks Aren't an Afterthought

The shoes you choose for backpacking are important. Almost as important are the socks you choose to go inside these shoes. A good sock should provide cushioning, protect your feet from abrasions, wick away moisture effectively and maintain an ideal temperature.

Cotton socks do not do this. In fact, cotton is a bad choice for anything in your pack because when it absorbs moisture it loses its ability to maintain a consistent temperature, loses its shape and becomes wrinkled (which often leads to blisters). Cotton also takes forever to dry compared to other materials.

The best choice for hiking socks is wool. Wool is light, fluffy and capable of maintaining a consistent temperature even when wet. This is especially important for cold weather hiking or times when you may have to cross streams, creeks or small rivers during your walk.

Specifically, the best socks are made from Merino wool. This material is more expensive than even many of the newer synthetic options, but it is well worth the cost.

It may seem like an inconsequential accessory but I assure you that skimping on your socks is not a good idea. After all, at best you will have two pairs (the one on your feet and one extra). Get something comfortable that can be rejuvenated with a quick dip in some cold water along the trail when they need a quick freshening up. Merino is also less smelly after a few days on the trail compared to other wool blends — something you and your hiking companions will definitely appreciate during the trip.

Some of the wool/synthetic hybrid socks work extremely well too. Synthetic fibers tend to be more durable and are usually found in the toe and heel areas and can greatly increase the longevity of your socks.

Regardless of which material you choose, make sure to keep dry socks on your feet. Wet socks make your feet soft and prone to blistering. A blister on the trail is not a fun experience. Either switch out the socks or take a break to let them dry whenever they become waterlogged or excessively wet from sweat.

One final note about socks: choose socks based on the conditions you expect. Heavy wool socks have no place in your bag for a summer weekend excursion but the dangers of frostbite are quickly realized when too thin of a sock is chosen for cold weather hikes.

Kicking It At Camp

Another footwear consideration is comfort shoes when in camp. The best option is a pair of cheap flip-flops. Made of thin foam and plastic, these type of shoes only weigh about three ounces and allow your feet to breathe after a day on the trail while protecting your feet from sharp objects around camp.

Although we aren't focusing on cold weather backpacking, you could easily switch out flip-flops for a pair of insulated booties for wandering around camp in the cold.

Either option takes up very little space and is a welcome treat after a long day. Believe me when I tell you that your feet will appreciate it.

Chapter Four: The Heart of Your Equipment

Recent years have provided backpackers with tons of options when it comes to the pack on your back. Second in importance only to the footwear you have selected, a pack is what gets your gear from camp to camp.

A good pack should be durable, lightweight (but made to carry the intended load) and comfortable on your back. As I mentioned earlier, you probably only need one pack to start so you should look for something large enough for long treks but small enough for a quick weekend getaway. If you find that you enjoy backpacking as much as I hope you do, you may decide to purchase specialized packs in the future depending on the type of trip you are planning.

Choosing the Perfect Pack

With so many choices available it may seem like a daunting task to choose just one pack that can meet your backpacking needs in the foreseeable future. Yes, there are lots of choices but for our purposes they all fall into two categories: ultralight frameless packs and lightweight internal frame packs.

Gone are the days of the external frame pack. You've probably seen them before — a large metal frame with a fabric pack attached. Although there are still a few companies that make these packs, it's not the type of design best-suited for getting into backpacking.

An ultralight frameless pack is just what the name implies. They are relatively small and typically designed for loads no greater than 20 pounds. They have no frame (although some may have a frame sheet for added support) and often have no hipbelt or padding. Ultralight packs are very popular with minimalist backpackers who enjoy traveling through the wilderness with as small a load as possible.

While these packs are usually inexpensive and a good choice for quick two day trips, the small size and limited features make them difficult to use for longer trips where more gear is required.

Lightweight internal frame packs are relatively new in the backpacking scene but have quickly been adopted by most backpackers. These packs come in a variety of sizes ranging from 2,500 - 5,000 cubic inches (40 - 82 liters) and can carry loads up to 45 pounds. The internal frame is usually nothing more than two metal strips that run through the pack and a frame sheet (usually made from plastic) to provide additional rigidity and balance.

Most lightweight packs are padded and usually come equipped with a hip belt which can move up to 90% of the weight off your shoulders. Never underestimate the power of a well-designed hip belt when shopping for a lightweight pack.

This is the category of pack best suited for the novice. In fact, I use a lightweight pack for just about every trip I take and always seem to have enough room to carry what I need. Look for something with at least 3,500 cubic inches of space if you plan to take longer trips. I use a 4,200 cubic inch pack that weighs approximately four pounds. Although it is certainly overkill for an overnighter, it has enough space to carry two weeks worth of gear and supplies when needed. For this reason, it is definitely the most versatile pack I own.

Size Matters

Just as it is important to ensure your footwear fits properly, it's important to select a pack that fits you well. If you go for an ultralight pack this isn't as much of a concern, but the lightweight internal frame pack is designed for a specific torso size.

Unlike footwear, however, the difference between manufacturer sizes isn't much so it's likely that a specific size pack from one brand should be very similar to the same size from a different brand.

I mention this in case you decide to purchase your pack online but choose to try a few on at the local store first.

A good pack isn't cheap so it helps to look for clearance items (like last year's model). Often you can get 50% off retail if you don't mind shopping around a little bit.

To find the right size pack for you, measure from the seventh cervical vertebrae (near the base of the neck) to the iliac crest (upper hipbone area). Although you can do this yourself, it is much easier to have someone help you. In a retail setting the staff can assist you with properly taking this measurement to ensure the best fit.

You must make sure the hip belt fits properly too. Our shoulders are not designed to carry large amounts of weight directly. The hip belt moves most of the weight away from the shoulders assuming it fits correctly.

Also, when trying on packs make sure they are loaded with at least 20 pounds of gear. An empty pack always feels like it fits and is a poor indicator of how the pack will feel when loaded down. Most outdoor shops will fill the pack for you so you can ensure it fits when loaded. I've even known some backpackers who bring their own gear in when shopping for a new pack to make sure the gear fits and the pack is comfortable.

Packing Up

Once you've decided on an appropriate pack, you need to make sure it is packed properly. This is something you will do every day when breaking camp so you might as well start practicing now.

The goal is to keep heavy items close to your back to maintain your center of gravity while walking. Most internal frame packs have a compartment on the very bottom designed for the sleeping bag. This keeps the bag protected and close to your body.

Before filling the main compartment, many people choose to put in a pack liner which could be as simple as a large plastic trash bag. By placing items inside the liner, they are reasonably protected from rain or an unexpected dip in the creek while crossing.

Start adding gear to the main compartment remembering to keep heavy items close to your pack and balanced from side to side to ensure an even load on the trail. Few things are more aggravating than walking miles with a lopsided pack.

Everything should fit in the pack with the exception of a few items you need easy access to such as a camera (mine goes in one of the hip belt pockets) or items that are too bulky to fit inside (such as a closed cell foam sleeping pad). Sleeping pads can be rolled tightly and lashed underneath the lid of the pack or if you use an inflatable pad, it can be stuffed in the main pack compartment with everything else (deflated and neatly folded of course).

While packing, also keep in mind when each item is to be used. The tent, for instance, should be near the top so you can quickly make camp in the evening. Insect repellent, sun screen and first aid items could be needed at any time so they should be relatively close to the top for easy access as well. Many packs have small outside pockets perfect for carrying these items.

Accessories to Consider

When it comes to carrying your gear, there are a couple of accessories you should consider that make protecting gear much easier. I already mentioned using a plastic trash bag as a pack liner, but a better solution is to use waterproof stuff sacks. Relatively inexpensive and lightweight, stuff sacks keep gear separated while protecting them from water.

This is especially important if you have rain gear or a wet tent fly you want to keep separate from dry gear in the pack. Carrying a couple of different sacks is a great way to keep your pack organized while protecting expensive items from water damage.

Some backpackers also use waterproof pack covers. Many newer packs actually come with these integrated into the lid of the pack. They are designed to cover everything and work well. The only problem with these is that they must be removed to access the pack — potentially allowing water to get into the pack as well.

Ideally, a quality pack cover and waterproof stuff sacks should be used to separate gear and protect it from the elements.

Chapter Five: Don't Forget Your Hat!

There is a well-known quote by an unknown backpacker that says: "There is no such thing as bad weather, only unsuitable clothing." This person couldn't be more right. As a backpacker, we encounter varying weather conditions all the time; especially when making rapid elevation changes. Daytime hiking weather could be in the 70's or 80's only to have the nighttime temperature drop near the freezing mark.

For this reason, it's important to dress appropriately for your trip and to understand the weather conditions likely to be encountered throughout different legs of the journey.

Before getting into how to dress for various weather conditions, it's important to understand how the body loses heat. Hypothermia can set in quickly as can heat exhaustion if we don't carefully control the heat of our own bodies.

The four ways our bodies lose heat are:

Convection is the transfer of body heat into the air. This is the most common cause of heat loss when backpacking and occurs when the air is colder than our nominal body temperature of 98.6° (which is most of the time). The faster cool air moves across our skin, the faster convection takes away body heat. This means clothing should be windproof.

Conduction is the transfer of heat from one surface to another. Since air is a poor conductor of heat, the best way to keep warm is to wear fabrics that trap the warm air near the body. Water, on the other hand, is an excellent conductor of heat. When clothes become wet they can quickly suck the heat away from the body. Backpacking clothing should be waterproof while still allowing sweat vapor to escape.

Evaporation is when body moisture (sweat) is transformed into a vapor resulting in a cooling effect. Clothing should transport this excess moisture away quickly through breathable membranes and vents that can be opened and closed to regulate moisture buildup and temperature as needed.

Finally, *radiation* is the transmission of heat between two objects without affecting the space between. This is how the sun warms us and if we aren't careful we can become overheated. Very little heat is lost by radiation, but wearing tightly woven and smooth clothing blocks most of the effects of radiation anyway.

Using Layers

Weight is an important factor when choosing clothing as is the clothing's ability to keep us warm and dry. The layer system is a way to accomplish all of this while maintaining ideal body temperature in a variety of conditions.

Instead of wearing one or two thick layers, we can wear three, four or even five layers (especially on the torso) to keep warm and shed some of these layers when it's warm. Often you will find that you have to add and remove layers multiple times throughout the day to maintain a comfortable temperature.

In its simplest form, a proper layer system consists of a thin inner layer of moisture-wicking material, a slightly thicker mid layer designed to trap warm air (insulation) and a waterproof but breathable outer shell that allows perspiration to pass through while blocking wind and rain. You can also add more mid layer clothing items as needed for especially cold weather. The point is that multiple thin layers of clothing is much better for backpacking than one or two thick layers.

The inner layer is only designed to remove moisture from the skin. Usually these are synthetic materials designed to wick moisture away from the body but even these materials can become saturated. The mark of a good inner layer is how quickly it dries out once removed. You do not want to put a damp inner layer near your skin on a brisk morning — it isn't comfortable or fun.

Midlayers have traditionally been made of cotton or wool but since the introduction of fleece both cotton and wool have all but disappeared from the trails. Fleece is warm, dries quickly and is very light compared to other options. A quality inner layer and fleece mid layer are sufficient to keep you warm in all but the coldest climates (especially when combined with a breathable windproof/waterproof outer shell).

Since you are just starting out, this should be sufficient clothing to keep you warm and dry. As you become more experienced and attempt winter backpacking trips, a down jacket, thick gloves and a wool hat should be added to your gear collection too.

As far as legwear is concerned, shorts are your best bet for mild weather hiking. They are lightweight, comfortable and usually have pockets useful for storing small items on the trail. As long as your upper body is warm, you might be surprised how comfortable shorts can be even in cool weather. This is mostly true while hiking — you may find your legs cold once you camp for the night.

A lightweight pair of hiking pants is a good idea as they can be slipped over your shorts in camp or when the weather is colder than expected. Jeans are a bad idea because they are heavy, uncomfortable and take forever to dry.

You shouldn't need a moisture-wicking inner layer for your legs unless you plan to backpack in cold or very wet weather but they are small and light enough that it's not a bad idea to bring them with you just in case.

Your Mom Was Right

When your mom shouted to you that you needed a hat on because it was cold outside, she wasn't trying to give you a hard time.

You really do need to wear a hat when you are even slightly cold. As much as 80% of body heat can be lost through the capillaries in the head because they do not constrict when cold like in other parts of the body. Essentially, if your feet are cold, put on a hat. Cold feet is a sign that your body is getting too cold so it is shutting down the blood flow to extremities in an effort to keep your brain and torso full of warm blood.

No matter what the weather, you should also carry at least a lightweight fleece hat just in case the evening temperatures are colder than you expected. Of course, if you plan on backpacking in the winter you want to invest in a heavy-duty wool or fleece hat that is comfortable enough to wear all day.

You should also consider a hat designed to keep the sun off your face and head in extremely hot weather. Even something as simple as a ball cap is better than nothing, but many hikers choose something with a brim that goes all the way around the hat for even protection from the sun's intense heat. Hats are also a great way to keep a bug net in place — something else you should consider because in some places the bugs can be absolutely relentless.

Proper backpacking clothing dictates that we assess the weather conditions likely to be encountered during the trip and implement the layer system using gear designed for the rigors of the trail.

Chapter Six: "Gimme Shelter"

In an ideal world we could sleep under the stars every night. Not only do backpacking shelters often shield us from the very thing we are trying to connect with, but they can weigh a lot and be difficult to erect in bad weather or in the dark after a long day on the trail.

I've spent many a night with the stars being the only roof over my head. In that time, I've been pretty lucky. Once I woke up nearly face to face with a hungry raccoon and a few times I woke up with spiders in my sleeping bag that I could have done without meeting. Other than that, it's been pretty uneventful. Stories abound, however, of backpackers sleeping with only a sleeping bag only to wake up to the sting of a scorpion, the bite of a snake or the creepy crawling of some large insect.

Not to mention that if the weather suddenly changes you could wake up with cold rain drops on your face!

For these reasons, bringing some form of shelter on your trip is a good idea. It could be as simple as a tarp or a bivvy bag or as elaborate as a fancy tent. Either way, just remember that you must carry your shelter with you so keep weight in mind while you assess the comfort and security of different shelters.

Simple Shelters

Simple shelters are lightweight, easy to set up and provide at least some protection from the critters and the elements. I classify both bivvy bags and tarps as simple shelters.

A bivouac bag, or bivvy bag, is nothing more than a waterproof sleeve you slide your sleeping bag into. Most bivvy bags have a hood that zips in place to keep water and bugs off your face. Bivvy bags are great because they are small, waterproof and still provide much of the "sleeping under the stars" experience. The downside is there is no room to move around or sit up so if you're forced to weather a rain storm you have no way to hang out, read or anything else.

Still, bivvy bags are small enough that it's not a bad idea to carry one as an emergency shelter even if you have another option in your pack.

Tarps are another shelter method that work well in mild weather. When constructed properly using trees, guylines and/or trekking poles, a tarp can be configured in many different ways from a basic lean-to to an A-frame ridge tent. Tarps provide protection from the wind and rain and can be set at a height allowing you to sit up. This means you can cook, read or relax in relative comfort.

The problem with tarps is they provide no bug protection (although some manufacturers sell bug screens for use with tarp shelters) and you are still at least partially exposed to the elements. Especially in cold weather this can be a serious problem.

If you decide to carry a tarp. something around 7' x 11' is more than sufficient. Two people could sleep under a tarp this size or one person with gear could sleep comfortably. It's large enough to allow multiple configurations but doesn't take up much space and only weighs a few ounces. Using a tarp you will also need high-quality stakes, rope and possibly trekking poles to erect the tarp depending on landscape. These items add weight but still usually not as much as a traditional tent.

Tents

I oversimplified bivvy bags and tarp shelters for one reason: I believe that you will enjoy your backpacking experience much more by adding a tent to your gear. No, I'm not talking about one of these

12 person "tent mansions" you see at local campsites and RV parks. A regular 1-2 person tent designed for backpacking is all you need. By shopping around, it's entirely possible to find a decent three season tent that weighs about five pounds including stakes and the rain fly. Not bad for decent shelter that keeps you bug-free and dry in a variety of conditions.

Modern tents are usually a two-wall design. This means the inner layer has mesh on the roof (perfect for stargazing in good weather) and a waterproof rain fly that goes over the top for additional warmth and protection from the elements.

When the weather is nice, you don't even need the rain fly but it's easy enough to put on when the weather turns on you.

When shopping for tents, you might be tempted to purchase one of the instant setup models. While I agree they are extremely easy to setup even in bad weather, they are typically about 25% heavier than the ones that require some assembly at camp every night. With practice, these tents can be setup in no time and the additional weight savings cannot be undervalued.

The biggest thing to consider when shopping for a tent is breathability. You want the material to be waterproof (for obvious reasons) but if there is no way for condensation to escape you could wake up soaked in water even on a dry night.

Condensation isn't a problem if the rainfly isn't used but when it is the condensation gets trapped on the rainfly. This moisture is supposed to be evaporated by airflow between the two layers but if there is no wind you often wake up with a rainfly soaked in water. No big deal except that it needs to be dried before breaking camp or at the very least put into a waterproof stuff sack so as not to get everything else in the pack wet.

Regardless of which brand tent you ultimately purchase, spend the extra few bucks to buy a bottle of seam sealer. Although most of the newer bathtub-style floor tents are reasonably waterproof from the factory, for ~$8 you can ensure the seams don't fail if the weather is really wet. It only takes a few minutes to apply seam sealer and it works wonders (even on cheap tents that are only water-resistant from the factory).

Whenever possible look for a tent with aluminum poles. Although typically more expensive, the weight savings of aluminum instead of fiberglass makes a huge difference. Remember, weight is everything when it comes to backpacking.

Also, take the time to try out your tent before actually taking it out on the trail. Set it up and take it down at least a couple of times so you become intimately familiar with how it works. It may not seem like a big deal until you're caught in a rainstorm. Setting up the tent as quickly as possible in those situations definitely makes the rain more bearable.

Finding a Campsite

Most popular backpacking trails have designated camping sites along the trail where most people choose to set up camp for the night. By examining these sites when you find them you quickly learn what makes a good campsite. Mostly, you want level ground free of standing water, rocks and other debris. If you are using a tarp for shelter you also want to look for a site with nearby trees that can be used when setting up the tarp.

It can be hard to find a campsite that is perfectly level. If you must sleep at a slight incline, make sure your head is uphill (it will be much more comfortable). What I like to do is lay down on the ground before pitching the tent to check the area. This is also a great way to detect sharp objects on the ground that could puncture or otherwise damage your tent.

Also take into account the weather. If it's very windy or rainy, seeking shelter under or near trees can be a good way to break up the weather. That said, high winds often knock branches from trees — a potentially hazardous situation when sleeping in a tent. Take this into account when selecting a site.

Staying Safe

In addition to staying away from trees with dead branches, you should also keep in mind some of the other hazards that can affect your campsite. For instance, lightning can be a hazard during certain seasons. Avoid making camp in a large open area or above the tree line if the possibility of thunderstorms is present.

Storms can also present another risk in desert climate zones — flash floods. Be weary of camping in narrow canyons or other areas where flood waters have obviously eroded the land. A storm could be hundreds of miles away in the mountains and still create flash flood conditions in the desert below. Always be aware of your surroundings.

Sleeping Bags

The goal of your sleeping bag is to trap heat while releasing moisture vapor to keep you warm all night. Sleeping bags come in many varieties that use different materials, fill weights, etc. depending on the use.

The fill of the bag is one consideration. You can choose from synthetic or down-filled bags. Although synthetic fill is usually less expensive and works better when wet, nothing can replace the warmth and compression ability of a down sleeping bag. What's more, down bags tend to last for at least 12 years while synthetic bags only last around four years (assuming regular use). If you don't mind paying a little more for a down bag and store it in a waterproof stuff sack to keep it dry, it is definitely the way to go.

The shell of the bag should also be considered but isn't nearly as important as the fill. This is especially true with down stuffed bags because they are almost always high quality (down is too expensive for manufacturers to justify cutting corners with the rest of the bag).

The size of the sleeping bag is also important. Mummy bags are popular because they work well at trapping heat close to your body. While rectangular bags give you more room inside the bag, they leave too much empty space which is quickly filled up with cold air. Find a bag that fits your body if you plan on camping in areas where the nighttime temperature is cold to maintain body heat throughout the night. Waking up shivering is no fun at all.

Chapter Seven: The Backcountry Kitchen

Food is necessary for our survival and in the backcountry it is one of the simple pleasures we can enjoy after a long day on the trail. There are many schools of thought when it comes to eating in the wilderness. Some people go all out baking breads using field ovens. These people usually aren't there to cover a lot of ground and often spend multiple days at a single campsite.

Other backpackers are of a survival eating mentality. They eat mostly cold foods and possibly a dehydrated hot meal for dinner.

There are benefits to both ways but I find that most hikers fall somewhere in between these two extremes. And believe it or not, many of the dehydrated camping meals are really good so don't discount them as a legitimate source of hot food on the trail.

As backpackers we need three main types of nutrition on the trail: fat, protein and carbohydrates.

Fats release energy slowly and can be used by the body when needed. They are not a quick source of energy so they are best saved for the evening meal. The energy from fat slowly releases during the night and helps keep you warm.

Protein repairs muscle and other body tissue. Eating protein throughout the day provides some energy but more importantly, it gives your body the fuel it needs to repair itself from the abuse of the trail.

Carbohydrates are immediately converted into energy and should be a staple of your diet. Simple carbs (i.e. sugars) give you a quick boost of energy and make for good trail snacks but the energy is spent quickly. Complex carbs (i.e. grains and vegetables) provide more energy over a longer period of time.

As a general rule while backpacking, your diet should consist of approximately 60-70% carbohydrates with the remaining amount spread out between protein and fats.

How Much Food to Take

I could bore you with all the scientific data regarding how much of which types of food you should take backpacking, but it's a waste of time. Most of us can't remember that boring kind of information anyway.

So let's make it simple: you should plan on bringing approximately 32 ounces of food for every day on the trail. For very short trips (1-2 nights) you could probably get by on half of this although you would be hungry most of the time. Longer trips demand proper nutrition and 32 ounces of food per day seems to be about right.

You may find that you need slightly more or less food to be comfortable while hiking and that's fine. I assure you, however, that if you plan on 32 ounces of food per day you will not starve and you may even find that you can reduce this amount slightly based on your own body's needs.

Keep in mind that this amount of food weight also includes condiments, powdered drinks and other small food items; not just the main course.

What to Eat

Remember that carbohydrates should constitute the majority of the trail diet. Everyone has their own preference when it comes to meal selection but we can make some generalized recommendations that definitely work well for most backpacking trips.

Breakfast

For some, breakfast can be as simple as some trail mix. It's quick, easy and doesn't require using the stove. Most people prefer something a little more substantial, however, and instant oatmeal is an excellent choice. It comes in a variety of flavors and is extremely lightweight. The hot water needed to make oatmeal can also be used to make a hot cup of tea, coffee or cocoa as well. There are also freeze-dried backpacker breakfasts including eggs and bacon that can be reconstituted with water and taste decent, but I try to keep freeze-dried meals to dinner if possible.

Lunch

Lunch is usually just a snack. Depending on the terrain you may not even decide to stop. Having a selection of trail mix, granola bars and an occasional chocolate treat are a good lunch especially if you are focused on making good time throughout the day.

Some people choose to get a little more fancy for lunch and eat sliced salami and cheese or similar items. On short trips, fresh fruits are also a good lunch time selection.

Dinner

This is the most important meal of the day and the one you will likely be looking forward to most during those last couple hours on the trail each day. Once camp is setup you can spend a little more time preparing this meal and some backpackers get very creative.

To keep things simple we will stick with freeze-dried hiking meals. There are plenty of meals to choose from so you can eat something different every night of the week. Since they are freeze-dried they take up very little weight or space and by adding boiling water they are ready to eat in a matter of minutes.

Other options are macaroni and cheese, instant mashed potatoes and Ramen noodle soup packets. All of these are light and provide a reasonable amount of trail nutrition although I find these items are usually best with other things added in for additional heartiness. Adding margarine, for instance, adds fat to the meal.

There are tons of other options available but these work for most people and with the exception of the freeze-dried meals are all inexpensive.

Packaging

Plastic bags are your friend. They compress to take up almost no space when not in use and can store pretty much any food item you bring along. Using plastic bags allows you to ditch the packaging most food comes in; an important concept when it comes to packing out your trash. Once the food in a plastic bag has been used up, the empty bag can be stuffed pretty much anywhere in your pack until you exit the wilderness and can dispose of it properly.

Critter Troubles

Pretty much every mammal and bird encountered in the wild would love to help you eat your food. That's why it's so important to store your food properly while in camp.

Most of us immediately think of bears. Yes, bears are a problem in areas where they are present. They can destroy your gear, your tent or anything else between them and an easy meal with a single stroke of the paw. But even in areas where bears are not present, mice and raccoons are especially troublesome.

Avoiding problems from these animals is usually as simple as keeping your pack in the tent with you at night. If bears are in the area, however, do not do this! You can hang your food from a tree, but some bears and raccoons have become extremely good at getting to the food anyway.

It is for this reason that I always store food in a bear-proof canister. Although they can be bulky to pack, they are actually required in many popular hiking areas and even in places where they aren't required I find that I would rather carry the canister then take a chance of losing my food to any critter.

Recently, a new product known as the Ursack (a bear-resistant stuff sack) came to market and it apparently works very well. I haven't tried it personally and many areas still require an actual canister, but it's certainly lighter and easier to pack than a canister. Especially if you are far from civilization, it's important to protect your food or else risk cutting your trip short when it gets taken.

Also keep in mind that bears cannot distinguish between scented food and non-food items. This means toothpaste, sunscreen and insect repellent should all be stored in your bear canister as well.

Always Know Where Water Can Be Found

A lack of water will kill you well before a lack of food will. At over 8 pounds per gallon, we can only feasibly carry a small amount of water at any given time. This means we need to know where water resupply points can be found throughout the hike.

In many places, finding sources of fresh water isn't difficult at all. There are rivers, lakes, streams and creeks all around. In arid climates, however, it could be miles and miles between water sources meaning you need to plan on carrying much more water than would normally be required.

What You Thought You Knew About Purification

There are going to be a lot of people who disagree with me on this one, but in most cases, purifying water while backpacking in the United States isn't absolutely necessary. Multiple studies have been done that prove this theory including one in the Sierra Nevada that basically said you would have to drink over 250 gallons of unpurified water to consume enough Giardia cysts to actually make you sick.

Purifying water with iodine is effective but takes time and makes the water taste horrible. Boiling water works well but it also takes time and uses up precious stove fuel.

There are also pump filters that do a reasonable job of filtering water but they take up a fair amount of pack space and can be extremely tiring to use.

If anything, I recommend carrying one of the new UV purifiers. Yes, they run on batteries that can run out but they work well and the water still tastes great afterward. If water is cloudy, you can pour it through a cotton bandana or coffee filter to remove most sediment (a necessity if using a UV purifier).

While most backpackers purify all water prior to consumption, I only do it if I'm forced to collect water from a source close to a popular campground or residential area where contamination is much more likely. Call me old-fashion, but there is something about drinking directly from a fresh mountain stream that prevents me from purifying water unless I have to.

Cooking on the Trail

Lots of people have a vision of cooking food over an open fire. While that's great in some instances, it is illegal in many popular hiking destinations unless you are at a designated campground with purpose-built fire pits.

Campfires also go against the Leave No Trace policy followed by most backpackers.

You're better off using a small camping stove for cooking. The risk of starting a wildfire is much lower and it's easier to control the temperature of the food as well. There are many schools of thought when it comes to which stove is best. My recommendation would be to use an alcohol stove in mild weather. They are small, easy to use and work with denatured alcohol which can be found cheaply nearly anywhere.

For colder weather, a multi-fuel stove capable of running on gasoline is probably better. Gasoline is easy to find and these stoves burn much hotter than alcohol stoves (an important consideration when temperatures dip low).

You're also going to need a cooking pot and some utensils. Notice I said *a* cooking pot (singular). It's easy to walk into the store and buy one of these ready-made cookware kits. The reality is that you don't need more than one pot in most cases. If you follow the meal recommendations made earlier, one pot is all you need and all you should carry with rare exception.

And as much as I have pounded the importance of saving weight, it's not worth spending the extra money on a titanium cooking pot when you are first starting out. While it's nice to shave the extra few ounces from your pack, aluminum pots work well and are also lightweight. In fact, the aluminum pot I currently carry was found at a thrift store and has put up with years of abuse without a problem.

Utensils are simple. A spoon is usually all that's needed but if you think you need a fork and knife as well, there are good three piece sets available cheaply from a variety of outdoor companies.

Chapter Eight: Comfort and Safety

We have covered all the basic gear necessary for having a successful backpacking trip but what about all the little things we haven't talked about yet? Well...that's what this chapter is about.

Light

It may go without saying but light is necessary on the trail. The popularity of LED lights which are smaller and more energy-efficient than incandescent bulbs has made this part of backpacking easy. A single LED headlamp should suffice for most hikes. There are even attachments that turn the headlamp into a lantern for use in the tent at night.

Although some people still use a handheld flashlight, the headlamp keeps your hands free which is unbelievably important when making camp or cooking after sundown.

First Aid

It's advisable to take a basic first aid course before starting off on your first backpacking adventure. The Red Cross and the YMCA both offer decent courses covering basic first aid techniques.

In addition to learning the skills required, you should carry a first aid kit with at least basic supplies. It doesn't need to be anything too complicated but if possible should be a kit designed for backpackers. Many popular outdoor retailers sell kits for this purpose.

Keeping Clean

You might be surprised by how infrequently you need to bathe in the wilderness. Yes, you might get a little smelly but it's usually nothing a quick dip in some water can't fix.

About the only area you should definitely wash all the time is your hands. You are more likely to ingest Giardia or other pathogens by improper hand washing than from drinking unpurified water. And if you are going on a short hike of a only a few days, this is likely all you need to maintain yourself until you return to civilization.

Keeping your hands clean is easy. There a plenty of biodegradable soaps available that can be carried in the pack although I would caution that these still shouldn't be used near water sources. An even better solution is a small bottle of hand sanitizer. Sanitizer doesn't require water and because it is alcohol-based it can even be used to help start fires.

For the rest of your body, No-Rinse Bath Wipes are a good choice. They are larger than normal baby wipes and don't leave a residue on your skin. Usually this is enough to keep you fresh until you get home and take a much-needed shower.

Other items should include a toothbrush, small tube of toothpaste (remember to store it in a bear canister in bear country) and some moist wipes for general cleaning duties.

Finally, don't forget toilet paper because wiping with leaves is not any fun! If you take out the center cardboard tube the roll takes up much less space in your pack.

Sunscreen and Bug Spray

These are both necessities in the wilderness. The sun's rays are much more intense at high elevations and sunburn is a quick way to ruin your trip. Likewise, bugs can be really bad during certain seasons so a quality bug spray is a must.

Both of these items are usually scented so they should be stored with your food in a bear canister when necessary.

Some people have a reaction to DEET, a popular chemical used in bug spray. It also melts plastic so if you use a spray with DEET make sure it is stored away from items that could be damaged. There are other bug sprays available that do not contain DEET and might be worth considering instead.

Some insects, especially black flies, are impervious to bug spray. For these critters a bug net and tightly woven clothing are essential. You can learn more about the insects you are likely to encounter by researching the area where you plan to hike.

Electronic Devices

There are all sorts of electronic devices found on the trail these days from iPod MP3 players to smartphones used for GPS navigation. While hardcore backpackers may disagree with having some of these electronic gadgets on the trail there is no denying that some of them can be very useful or entertaining.

The Amazon Kindle, for instance, allows a backpacker to carry thousands of books in a small device no larger than a paperback book. Since I love to read in the tent in the evening, the Kindle is perfect for me.

Likewise, many people enjoy listening to music while loafing around camp at night. Smartphones and iPods work well for this.

I also bring my smartphone on the trail but only to use as a standalone GPS unit. I put the phone in Airplane Mode to conserve battery and the app I use allows me to map my progress in real-time. It works well and in an emergency I could call for help on the phone assuming there was a signal.

Cameras are another popular device and are a great way to document your trip along the way. Many backpackers are semi-professional photographers who have honed their skills through years on the trail. Hence, these people tend to have expensive DSLR cameras. Personally, I have a basic point-and-shoot with optical zoom that fits perfectly into one of the pockets on my hip belt. It takes pretty good pictures and works well for my purposes.

No matter what electronics you decide to bring, you need a way to charge them if you are going to be traveling for more than a day or two. Fortunately, there are quite a few lightweight solar chargers available. Usually, these units strap to the outside of your pack allowing you to charge necessary items while you hike. Obviously they do not work well (or at all) on cloudy days or when you are in deep forested areas with little sunlight but they are a welcome addition to the average backpacker's gear list.

Chapter Nine: Navigation

I saved this chapter for last for two reasons. First, navigation is extremely important so I want to make sure you remember it. Second, it can seem a little overwhelming for novice backpackers so I didn't want to scare you off from this rewarding pastime before you have time to give it a fair shake. Nobody wants to get lost in the woods, but with a little practice that shouldn't be a concern for you.

I will say that navigating using a map and compass is easy once you know how to do it. Using modern technology such as GPS (either standalone or on a smartphone) makes navigation even easier. Also, if you plan to hike well-worn trails in the beginning (which you definitely should) you may find that traditional navigation tools are practically unnecessary. The trails are well-defined and there are usually plenty of signs and other markers showing you the way.

You can practice your navigational skills on these types of trails so when you find yourself in an unfamiliar place in the future you know how to find your way to where you want to be.

Maps

Every backpacker needs to understand how to use maps properly. A good map is often all you need to navigate successfully on the trail and it certainly makes planning your trip much easier.

You can start using online tools like Google Maps to give you a good overview of a particular area where you want to hike. Once you have narrowed down your hiking area, the best thing to do is order specific maps for that area through local resources such as the Bureau of Land Management or the National Park Service (depending on where you are going).

Topographical maps are a great way to estimate the elevation changes you are likely to encounter on the trail and planimetric maps are useful for picking out certain features along a trail such as junctions, water sources and other useful information.

There are also excellent maps available from private sources including National Geographic. These maps often include more detailed trail information than typically found in maps from public sources. Usually a combination of different maps is the best way to get a good idea of what you will encounter on the trail. Many of these maps can also be downloaded to your computer, smartphone or standalone GPS unit for easy navigation on the trail. This is especially helpful because you can mark water sources and other waypoints before even setting foot on the trail.

Compass

Although a combination of good maps and a GPS unit make a compass obsolete, they are inexpensive and lightweight so you should have one and know how to use it in case other navigational aids fail.

A simple orienteering compass is all you need. These are nice because they can be placed directly on a map to determine direction based on your current location.

Compasses are useful when you are forced to travel across large open spaces where a trail may not be clearly marked. They are also helpful in bad weather when GPS units may not be accurate and visibility is limited.

GPS

I like using GPS even if some backpackers don't agree. They make navigation extremely easy and I can mark important areas along my route before I even leave my house. As a novice backpacker, I suggest using GPS to make navigation easier and practically worry-free.

The apps available for most popular smartphones work well as long as you have a solar charger to keep the phone running for the duration of the trip. Standalone units usually boast better battery life but they can be expensive. Which way you decide to go is up to you. I just use my smartphone for this purpose but I still carry a good map of the area and a compass just in case.

Trail Markers

Popular trails often have plenty of signs along the way to assist hikers navigating through the wilderness. Most often these signs are found at junctions (where multiple trails intersect) but sometimes you will find them along the trail as well.

More common along the trail, however, are makeshift markers usually made by other backpackers. This is especially common along rocky parts of the trail where the path may not be clear.

Markers can be small piles of rocks (known as cairns or ducks), blazes on trees, paint on trees or rocks, makeshift signs and metal badges nailed to trees. There are other markers as well but these are the most common.

While you should never add any markers of your own (sometimes this is considered vandalism), it does help you navigate difficult trail sections where the way may not be totally clear. Keep your eyes out for these markers as you hike.

Conclusion

The information above covers most of the major questions usually posed by novice backpackers. Gear selection and weight reduction are often overlooked aspects of hiking but I think you now have a pretty good understanding of just how important these facets of backpacking are.

Navigation is also important as is planning your trip well before you even think about stepping into the wilderness. While you are more likely to be injured while driving to the trailhead than you are while actually on the trail, accidents do happen and people do get lost.

My hope is that you take the information in this guide and apply it to your backpacking adventures. It is nearly impossible to describe the feeling of becoming one with the wilderness. The only way to understand and appreciate the phenomenon is to get out there and do it yourself.

Is backpacking difficult? Yes.

Is it worth the time and effort required to do it safely? Absolutely!

Without a doubt, few things are as rewarding in life as learning to survive in the wilderness. If you have made it this far in the book, you obviously have a desire to experience nature so the only thing left to do is get out there and start learning. I hope to see you out there!

Happy trails!

Appendix I: Gear Checklist

The checklist below includes all the gear you might possibly take on a backpacking trip. You would never take all of this gear for a single trip. Rather, you can go through this list to create custom gear lists for specific trip using the information you have learned throughout this book.

Packs

- [ ] Backpack
- [ ] Fanny Pack
- [ ] Day Pack

Footwear

- [ ] Hiking boots
- [ ] Trail shoes
- [ ] Sandals
- [ ] Flip-flops
- [ ] Socks
- [ ] Fleece socks
- [ ] Snow shoes
- [ ] Crampons
- [ ] Insulated booties
- [ ] Trekking poles
- [ ] Walking stick

Shelter

- [ ] Dome tent (with poles and stakes)
- [ ] Bivvy bag
- [ ] Tarp (7'x11')

- ☐ Groundsheet (if using tarp)
- ☐ Sleeping bag
- ☐ Sleeping pad

Cookware

- ☐ Stove
- ☐ Fuel
- ☐ Fuel containers/bottles
- ☐ Windscreen
- ☐ Pan
- ☐ Mug
- ☐ Plate or bowl
- ☐ Spoon
- ☐ Pot scrubber
- ☐ Water purification (UV, filter or chemical treatment)
- ☐ Water containers
- ☐ Matches, lighter or magnesium firestarter
- ☐ Bear canister
- ☐ Plastic ZipLoc bags
- ☐ Food (approximately 32 ounces per day)

Clothing

- ☐ T-shirt
- ☐ Shirt
- ☐ Long underwear
- ☐ Underwear
- ☐ Synthetic shirt
- ☐ Wool shirt
- ☐ Wool sweater
- ☐ Cotton shirt
- ☐ Fleece top
- ☐ Insulated top
- ☐ Windproof top

- ☐ Raingear
- ☐ Shorts
- ☐ Trail pants
- ☐ Fleece pants
- ☐ Sun hat
- ☐ Ball cap
- ☐ Wool hat
- ☐ Fleece hat
- ☐ Bandanna
- ☐ Liner gloves
- ☐ Wool or fleece mittens
- ☐ Shell mittens
- ☐ Insulated gloves

Miscellaneous

- ☐ LED headlamp
- ☐ Handheld LED flashlight
- ☐ Compass
- ☐ Maps
- ☐ First Aid Kit
- ☐ Safety Whistle
- ☐ GPS
- ☐ Hygiene kit (toothpaste, toothbrush, moist wipes, hand sanitizer)
- ☐ Sunscreen
- ☐ Bug repellent
- ☐ Head net
- ☐ Knife
- ☐ Scissors
- ☐ Toilet paper
- ☐ Rope
- ☐ Plastic bags
- ☐ Stuff sacks

☐ Entertainment devices (smartphone, Kindle, iPod, etc.)

18581896R10035

Made in the USA
San Bernardino, CA
20 January 2015